Praise for
Zone of Silence

In his poetry collection, *Zone of Silence*, Dario Beniquez sees his poems as a painter. He spreads his colors across a broad canvas, drawing images that are different from each other but blend well together. In "Who can Saves us Now?," he touches on the Mayan legend of worry dolls that absorb our worries, while "Brooks Air Force Base, 9/11" is a personal vignette about the 2001 terrorist attacks. Other poems deal with ghosts, PTSD, and aliens, leading readers to imaginative excursions, inviting them to consider new ideas. Beniquez's background shines through with his sprinkling of scientific language in his collection. *Zone of Silence* will appeal definitely to everyone!

— **Gil Dominguez**, author of
They Answered the Call: Latinos in the Vietnam War

Dario Beniquez's poems beckon us during a pivotal moment in the world's history. His poems mirror current surreal experiences that test and taunt the reality of human life. Beniquez commiserates with us, not necessarily guiding us, so much as providing companionship in an increasingly bewildering world. His poems confront existence, exposing a vulnerability that validates both meaningful and meaningless moments of life—they test and love the world at once. Like the protagonist in his poem, "Undisclosed Location" Beniquez translates "unreal to the real" grounding us as the world spins on testing our experience. *Zone of Silence* is anything but silence. Beniquez is the voice we need now to give us solace, and the work we will need in the future to understand the humanity of these uncertain times.

— **Claudia R. Guerra**, editor of
300 Years of San Antonio and Bexar County

This *Zone of Silence* is an exploration of world dynamics. The reader is confronted with images of war and social injustice: "[W]alls go up, walls crumple, large flags fly. (…) [B]orders break, towns burn, no one survives." The language is at the same time narrative and lyrical: "The moon is a skeleton. It's All Saints' Day. The zombie war won." There is a cinematic quality in these poems, an acute perception that reveals Beniquez's private universe: "Say that the shrapnel/missed me. (…) And I read poems I hope were true." In the middle of harsh realities, the author creates a space for understanding; he is brave enough to rescue the human connection: "In a migrant center, I hand out a box lunch/to a little boy drumming a cartoon tune."

— **Mariano Zaro**, author of
Decoding Sparrows

Zone of Silence

FLOWERSONG
P R E S S

poems by
Dario Beniquez

FLOWERSONG
PRESS

FlowerSong Press
Copyright © 2021 by Dario Beniquez
ISBN: 978-1-953447-81-4
Library of Congress Control Number: 2021946247

Published by FlowerSong Press
in the United States of America.
www.flowersongpress.com

Cover Art by Dario Beniquez
Cover Art Design by Connie Wong Beniquez
Set in Adobe Garamond Pro

for Dora Wong Kieou

CONTENTS

ONE

THREE

FOUR

They speak of the art of war,
but the arts
draw their light from the soul's well,
and warfare
dries up the soul and draws its power
from a dark and burning wasteland.

— **Denise Levertov, "Misnomer"**

ONE

Are We Not Safe Here?
(Mayan legend of the Worry People)

My friends worry obsessively.
They worry about the end of the world,
harmonic convergence, Mayan Cosmology, my retirement.

They persist on building bomb shelters,
steel-reinforced concrete bunkers, with a water supply
to last one hundred eighty days, can foods: Goya, De Monte,
frijoles, habichuelas, ten-pound bags of Mahatma rice, a shelf
with an RCA transceiver to pick up strayed communities.

They worry about me. Where's your bunker? Don't you care?

We can be attacked at any minute. Anthrax, biological weapons,
are everywhere; an earthquake can strike at any time, a tsunami
can send us scampering to the hills.

Then I think, I could be squashed by a baby grand piano falling from the
sky,
this minute or be infected with a wild virus, but I don't.

They worry for me, my friends. I worry for them, the worry people.
I carry them with me all the time, and at night, I place them underneath
my pillow and let them do the worrying for me.

Zone of Silence

"Are you lost?" asked the rancher on horseback.

"No, we are not," replied the visitors. "We are travelers from another world, outfitted with armored suits because fighting wars is what you do."

"Our mission is to discover how you survive with so many wars in process."

Later in the evening, 20,000 feet above the travelers' landing site, sonic booms shattered the silence; air-to-ground missiles penetrated the ground destroying the visitors and their spacecraft.

In the fighters' cockpits, green lights flashed on and off across the digital display—target hit, mission complete, target hit, mission complete....

They came not to invade us, but to save us.

Austere Airfield

(Southwest Asia)

"Who can I kill?" the sign read.
I thought it read, "Who can I heal?"

So I walked around with my hand
outstretched like a holy man,

attempting to heal the lame, blind,
and despondent—to no effect. But

I did not come here to heal,
but to search for a launching pad to hush

the incurable, the politically skewed,

to set them down on the righteous path
to democratic ends.

Brooks Air Force Base, 9/11

Ed Custodio, a contract specialist, runs into my cubicle, "You've gotta watch this!" he says. So like two strangers escaping a wildfire we rush into the first available conference room. On a TV screen, we see a man on a rooftop; behind him, a commercial plane crashes into a tower. The video plays over and over again like an unwanted hypodermic needle into our flesh.

Within seconds, the room jams up with workers frozen in space. Straightaway, Major Nicholson breaks up the spell, "Everybody, go home! We're evacuating the Base." Hundreds of people pour out the building, hundreds more race out the compound. But inside the dark building, I sought refuge under a desk just as I was taught at Public School 61 to "Duck and Cover," "Duck and Cover," when the bomb comes for us.

Rudy's Barbecue

In the late afternoon, in the anatomy lab,
I dissect a pig. I hold its purple

heart in my hand. I think to myself,
such an unholy act is this.

As I roll into my skin, into myself,
I think, do pigs go to heaven?

Then darkness overcomes light; the ground
swells beneath my feet, a flask shatters,
tiles crack.

Somewhere in a temple, a veil splits.

Next day, at Rudy's Barbecue
I forego my customary pulled pork sandwich,
order the brisket instead.

After lunch, I dissect another pig.

Lower East Side

In the mist of saltwater, I spit out waves that drown me. Rockaway, this beach engulfs me. Yet, I see Essex Street, the Lower East Side.

Inside the skeleton of a building, paint bleeds. I see an inkblot, America. I see the prohibition against lead-based paint—oh, the sweetness of disease.

In a tenement, a boy curls up in an armchair. Darkness overcomes light. There are monsters in this house, the mummy, the werewolf.

Eyes crawl walls. Shadows climb windows. Fire-escape rattles. Tiny bones shake.

Sometimes, I go back to the building where I lived. I look up through metal cages, fire-escapes, to my beginnings.

Unseen from the street, I step back and spot our window. I know I am there when I see pigeons circle the building. They cast a shadow over our place.

Red Lobster

Those of us who grow
beyond
        apple-green with age

know the truth about our cells—
        our hair gone.

Our heads sparkle in the sunshine
        or painted blonde to cover our age.

It feels so dandy to wake up
              to such a blind day.

Where have my shoes run to?
             Where are my keys?

What unholy doors do they unlock?
        Maybe, they've eloped to *Tahiti*.

Then the truth slaps my forehead,
           every moment yateky yaks
into dark matter.

Molecules juggle in my brain,
        form compounds of embarrassment.

Later,

        I see strangers waving at me
at Red Lobster.

Who are these faces, my
                  brain asks?

Up close, I extend my hand,
                  smile in gladness, and say,

Long time no see.

            Thinking,

Shoot, I never liked these people anyway.

Chicken Dance

I was born a question mark
to Jehovah, a cause célèbre, an anomaly,
a misplaced modifier in warp time,
laughing in the world.

Once, I saw a falling star
over Jamaica Bay

near my high school where years
later a plane from JFK
dropped from the sky leaving
no survivors.

I wanted to be an engineer to fix
things and that is exactly what I became,
inventing a Built-in-Test system,
a self-diagnostic algorithm
for aircraft line replaceable units.

Now buried in an IEEE database—
costs too much to retrieve.

I never thought I would have it so good,
living in Lancaster, dancing the chicken dance
at the edge of the road.

Who Will Save Us Now?

She jumped into our universe from where no one knew. Not even the detective with her sharp gray eyes knew. The tree trimmer with his rattling chainsaw simply stared at her, puzzled as heck why she was standing in front of the Safeway with two shopping bags.

Nonetheless, there she was pulling out facemasks, handing them out to pedestrians, shoppers, children, workers—an elderly woman with a hand-made sign with blue large letters that read, "Free Masks, Mascaritas, Masks. No Donations Necessary."

Every day without fail, snow, rain, or hail, she handed them out, surgical masks. Who was this woman? Was she an apparition from another planet, another dimension? Perhaps, Lucifer knew, but I doubted it.

She persisted, day after day, 30, 60, 90 days, an eternal supply of masks until the whole city wore masks, including children—their toys wearing tiny bandannas and handkerchiefs.

Everywhere masks dominated, on the streets, in the park, in the post office, even in backyards. This went on until the malicious virus was no more and the pandemic over. After that, the world was no longer the same, and she was no more.

Invisible City

In the town of El Paraiso cobblestone roads
spiral away from the equestrian statue of General Tomas Regalado,
and somewhere outside the settlement along the way roads vanish
into the sparse flowers of the volcanic soil.

And just off El Guayabo ridge where our house stood,
my grandfather singularly walked to the mission school.
There he learned about Joseph Smith,
about legions of angels, and ancient people who crossed
the ocean, who worshipped the one true God,
and how he *too* could live forever.

This was how my father and I became followers
of Elohim. But not my mother, she continued to believe
in the old ways and spirit guides. So always in the early morning
darkness, she would light candles
to the blindfolded saints of El Salvador.

She never gave up her faith, and upon her death; her collections of saints
were buried with her. However, it is in her custom
that I continue to exist and strive to find my way in the world.

El Hombre sin Ojos

The man-without-eyes
sits on a tropical island
looking towards a lagoon.

Pink & gray flamingos step
in and out of the swallow water.
Palm trees ride the wind.

But, he's actually
in a blue room facing a rocky river
in Hamilton, Ohio.

In the City of Aguadilla

every morning at 6:30 a.m.
an old man with green eyes, white mustache,
walking cane, circles the Spanish plaza

checking car license plates,
adding each one, one by one, to see
which ones add up to seven, those that don't
he forgets. He believes that one day

all the license plates on the Spanish plaza
will add up to seven, then a starship
will descend onto the city

and a being from another star system
will transform us into higher human beings

PSTD Cento

It was all in my mind. It was an idea I had!

Say that the shrapnel
missed me, I flew
back to the carrier, and every morning
take the train, my
hands on a black case, and sit
upright held
by the firm webbing.

And I read poems I hoped were true.
It's like been there, brother, been there.

I look about wildly.

And wonder just what in the hell I'm doing here
so many thousands of miles away from what I know best.

"Stop! It's a dream! It's a dream!"

And soldiers, they too are wounded.
They too are sifted from their loss
and are without hope. The core
softens. The pure flesh softens
and melts. There are thorns, there
are the dark seeds, and they end.

No Way to Die

I bury my toy soldiers,
for once and for all,
in the backyard.
Every Sunday,
I check on them.
I want to make
sure, they are safe
in their tiny coffins.
I want them
to stay there.
Yet when I think
of the number
of Armenians killed,
the killing fields where
bodies reside,
El Holocausto,
and the hundreds and thousands
yet to come,
the buried soldiers
rise, rise.
They inhabit flesh,
join the machinations
of tactical minds.
Then I think,
we may all vanish
in the shine of an eye
by a mere thumb's up.
There is no way
to bury the dead.

November 11, 2020

(After *Lyric in Time of War, American String Quartet*)

The dead speak. They talk to us in dreams,
tell us what we do not see, what we see,
on the TV screen.

How shall we end the army of explosives?

How shall we end the clouds of destruction?
Do we need a human cry?

The dead do not lie. They come back
like the knights of the dead to remind us
we are a step away from the army of the dead

or they come back to take our flesh,
to time us on their ghostly watches to see
how long it will take us to rise again.

Drones

Each drone targets the heart, each one of them
a gray eagle, a bouquet of missiles.

In a village, a boy punches a soccer ball
against a graffiti wall, a woman scrubs clothing in a basin,
a man pushes a wheelbarrow towards a wheat furrow.
A wall divides the village.

Near the wall, folks gather. Gray eagles saturate
the sky. Missiles strike. They vanish.

More drones cloud the sky. More fear clouds the soul.

The Void

When you open
       your eyes forever
don't be surprised
       to find out that hell
doesn't exist,
       and that heaven
is a state of mind,
       and that somewhere
there is a duplicate
       of you thanking
you for his or her
       existence.

Hello, Darkness, Hello

Isn't it funny how wars continue on whether anyone minds them or not? How they continue to exist like moons revolving around a dying star or an asteroid that gets 500, 300, 100, years nearer, closer, to earth, until the inevitable happens to the invincible ones, to the unbelievers in their colorful suits.

Who is to say, this is the beginning of the millennium or the end? Where is the promise of one thousand years of peace forecasted by the prophet? Who will save us now? The smooth sayers say, "It's up to me to be." Yet the stock market goes up and down its merry way. What will become of you or me?

The first plague strikes and flies away. We laugh. We drive our cars, eat out, and play ball. The plague spikes then takes away our nurses, soldiers, ministers, newborns, and a few more of us.

Nations oppose nations; walls go up, walls crumple, large flags fly. Drones darken clouds; the war flares up, borders break, towns burn, no one survives. Homeless dogs scavenge streets, more missiles strike warehouses, more money flows, high-rises rise, countries flourish, famish.

Somewhere in a grotto, ancient texts warn us the earth shall end in a big chill—everywhere glaciers will cover the masses, or in a big crush—continents will fold and unfold onto themselves. Other prognosticators think, perhaps, the world will end in a big blast,—fire raining down on civilians, upon forests, cities, mountains, and oceans.

Yet some believers believe all three will consume us. None of this may be true and potentially some novel toxin will wipe us out. But the "when," has past, and "now" is here. Who among us will stand-up to summon the angel of mercy?

No matter what, the universe shall bounce back and the cycle of new births shall continue with or without us.

Susquehanna River

Morning arrives like a possum,
the computer's screen an endless flatland,
each email a bundle

of desire, the office hallway, dark tunnels,
filled with workers racing by, avoiding
each other's eyes. I feel

like the character in Groundhog Day,
repeating the same day over and over

again. One day, I'll get it right. Project folders
clutter my desk, binders stacked high,
a project in Grand Fork, North Dakota—

four hundred Russian Cypresses to soak up
a toxic spill; another in North Carolina
to wipe out fungi in the aviators' quarters.

Projects scattered everywhere,
sixty-four voicemails await me—the operator,
oh, so courteous.

More projects, more contamination,
radioactive plumes in the Susquehanna river,
the earth growls.

Dali's Brain

Hegel was wrong. Everything he said was wrong about the swamp full of alligators. About Louisiana, he was wrong. He never really loved her. He never got her right. She left him.

His world was words, mostly abstractions, words of inimitable images. He woke up to the sky. The sky was full of indecipherable codes. The writing in the clouds was inappropriate, just a bunch of nonsensical symbols: flying spoons, tectonic dips, misshapen creatures—space waste from the liminal mind.

He thought he could find matter. He believed matter was secondary to intellect until he caught his finger on a kitchen drawer. Poor Hegel, all his writing, all his philosophizing, all his maps, and textbooks piled up in his backroom collecting mites.

Mites feasting on knowledge, praying until dawn, eating, because no one ever taught them to read. It was just food to them, nourishment to make their tiny brains grow. The brain a perplexing appendage, they surmised.

Engrossed in the turmoil of books, no mental institutions cared for them. No one knew their purpose, their smarts; no one thought about their brilliant work. Their job was to clean up the clutter, to make a path to enlightenment, to straighten up Hegel's untidy bookcases. What did they know about the approaching storm?

TWO

OWI

Tu También
(You Too)

Men don't get lonely; they get drunk
like my friend Corporal Carrasco.
A short stocky Puerto Rican,
who would go to the NCO club
to pick a fight.
He hated the Army.
His accent told it all,
a draftee from Rincón.
The easiest way out of this
man's army was to be classified
as maladjusted.
So he stayed angry, all the time.
He told me, everybody is a pendejo,
tu también.
That didn't bother me,
maybe, he was right.
It wasn't long before at reveille,
the sergeant shouted,
Carrasco!
Here! Aqui, pendejo.
Pack it up, soldier!
Off he went to Vietnam,
another brother down.

During the War

I was in Tent City—hundreds of trucks, armored cars,
tanks, copters, on a bare strip of land.

Gamers bombed a city, a desert, thousands of miles
away. Drones dominated airspace.

The War a liquid receding, deceiving,
an endless vortex; time a Mobius eclipse
in the green zone, target zone, real zone.

Pulsating waves transmitted digital details,
mountains, valleys, ammo depots, of enemy
sites to satellite transceivers in the heavens.

At night on my cot, I sent telepathic messages to my family
in Tennessee. "All is well."

Next day, a foul wind penetrated our camp,
like an invisible spear zooming through the sky,

a missile demolished the chow hall minutes after Miguel
and I had left from drinking tea.

After the attack, the troops cleared the debris; rattled nerves
slithered through the camp like chameleons in an attic.

Seekers

So I walk out into the universe to test my existence.

Why does worry preoccupy the city, the planet?

In the migrant center, I hand out a box lunch
to a little boy drumming a cartoon tune.

A mother sits on the floor, bottle-feeds a child.
She looks up at me. I give her two box lunches.

Souls in a strange land, different pace, a mortal time…

A man stands in a cold corner of the migrant center,
he carries a canvas tote bag, inside the bag, one short
sleeve shirt and dungarees.

He cautiously walks up to me and says, "Tengo hambre."
I reach for another box lunch.

The stench of God is everywhere, in the water, on the walls,
in the air.

The world spins on, the city stamps on. Migrants,
folks, knock on our doors.

Daughter

    She sings a song

No one hears

    She sings a song

She cannot hear —

    She sings a song across the years

Nena, daughter,

    Hija, I hear the song & sing

It with no return

    Yet in the travel of the stars,

In the echo of Monte Santo, the place

    Where the wind spoke to us, a song still

Resonates within me—there a bond was formed

    That even eternity cannot dissolve

On the Way to the Arecibo Observatory

to view the starry planets, on a narrow mountain road,
an Appaloosa stood in our path.

Pleasantly, she nibbled on a branch,
the patches on her coat formed constellations of distant worlds,
unknown stars of the Andromeda Nebula, tails of comets, galaxies
of butterflies.

In the dream space of my mind, I traveled to a mystical world,
saw Joshua trees in a neon desert, flowers that bloomed above the sea,
rivulets of lava that spilled into ice caves, flying reptiles
with diamond wings, starships descending and ascending beyond
a violet horizon.

And, in the pearl eyes of the Appaloosa, I saw the outer reaches
of space where earth revolves, like the ocean of stars that watch
our lives in the inquietude of our world.

Ghost Story

When I found you in Durango on a blanket
of bunchgrass, ants crawling over your arms, *you*
on your back, a ghost, separate,
a *fantasma*, dizzy with dismay, eyes shut,
you were unwilling to move.

You told me, you preferred the naked desert,
the occlusion of the mind, the painlessness
of the unknown world, the idleness of a crypt,
I refused to let you go.

So I picked you up and took you to your
apartment, sat you down on the bed, fed
you water, bits of pastry.

As you regained your disposition, I spoke
haltingly to you, about the emptiness
we all feel, about the incomprehensible

absence that you would create in her,
your child, and in her child. And how then
would she conquer the unknowable
fears after you've left?

And how difficult it would be for her
to carry-on in your stead when it is easier
for you to live than leave?

Then you pulled yourself up, stared silently
back at me, kissed a star around your neck,

and walked out the storm door towards
the dark Durango sky.

Undisclosed Location

When I went over there, we were at war.
The weather was wet and cold, temperature 30 degrees.

In Frankfurt, security agents said, "Take photos of everything.
Exercise caution. Your body is a loudspeaker."

Deployed, I was in an army tent with three fellows.
The language symbols masked with noise. The runway
unpaved, broken airfield lights populated its end.

Ahmad, the engineer, saw this.
His mind calculated the ratio of a runway strip to the target zone.

Ramón, an architect, an artist, painted on a steno pad
the landscape, storage sheds, an air control tower in repair,
troops in winter's shadows.

I translated the unreal to the real—lines on a map to roadways,
water towers, buildings, gunnery range, ammo igloos, bunkers.

Roger, a naval intelligence officer, the surveillance leader,
memorized vehicle movements, consolidated photos
and notes—reported to headquarters.

Back in Frankfurt, we briefed the colonels. Back in the States,
my mind settles nowhere…

In the Military

1

Late for work, I took a shortcut,
going as fast as I could through a wet farm road in New Mexico.

As the locals say, "You can easily disappear in the mud around here."
Indeed, I did.

Called Master Sergeant Schuller from the Heavy Equipment Shop.
He came out and pulled my small Subaru out with a yellow tow strap.
He said, "Here, keep the tow strap, in case you get stuck again."

One morning, the Military Police stopped me at the gate, and told me
to open up my trunk. They found the yellow tow strap, and turn me in
to the squadron commander, who reprimanded me for transporting
and using government property for personal use.

2

Almost 105 degrees, in the Mojave,
I walked into the Orderly Room,
with my field jacket unzipped and opened,
got stopped by the section commander,
had a little conversation with him,
and received an Article 15
for being out of uniform.

3

At Fort Dix while ETSing,

exiting out of the Army. I wound up
on the Details list for KP, kitchen police:
peeling potatoes, washing pots and pans,
mopping the chow hall. I told
the First Sergeant to go suck an egg.

In the Middle of the Night

Sometimes you wait up in the middle of the night. You know it's the middle of the night because that's when strange things happen, in the middle of the night, not the beginning or end of the night but the middle of the night. You get up from the bed drowsy, wander around the house looking for nothing in particular. After all, it's the middle of the night.

You open the closet door and are attack by boxes pile too high. An old trench coat stares threateningly at you. You check the house alarm and the light is still green. You check the backyard door. Secured. Then you decide to check inside the refrigerator. There may be something alive in there? A lobster or a giant squid. Nah. All you see is yesterday's leftover, straight from Jim's Restaurant, a half-eaten chicken fried steak, and a tiny plastic cup of corn. Not—hungry now.

Why are you up? What are you doing? Darn it! It's the middle of the night. You feel safe. You feel blessed. The whole world is blessed. Then you hear claws scratching on the living room window. You knew it! Something dreadful is about to happen. You crawl on your belly as you were taught during the army infiltration course, and slide towards the window. Peek through the curtains, and there it is, your neighbor's mesquite tree clawing at your window.

Okay, that's enough; you'll trim it, tomorrow.

Then you dream, somewhere in the Caribbean or Catalonia, your lost daughter pushes an empty carriage along a backroad in a dying fog.

Battle Fatigue

No angel comes for me.
I walk, and walk, and walk,
then run, and run, and run,

with no breath.

The sea extends before me,
a sheet of glass, a mirror to my past.

A child's voice whispers to me.

Everywhere is gone.

Fog lights call to me,

     We cannot see you.

The weather is so clear.
I can hear forever.
Stillness flames my fears.

I cannot breathe.
No angel comes for me.

I run on and on, and on.

War Secrets

Notes hit the ground tossing, turning, slipping.
The wind claws them with fingernails of fire,

rushes them to some undisclosed location, to some
underworld—notes of empty eyes, wet desert sand,
irises.

Hands frozen, ears icicles, jacket flapping, I track them
to the parking lot. I grab one, drop another, run after it,

open my briefcase,—throw the rest to the wind.

Door Gunner
(John Zavala of Rockaway)

I am not surprised if there
is a bullet with my DNA
etched on it.

Now, I walk twisted
as everyone sees.

My life's a shopping cart
things go in, things go out.

I am a soldier inside my grief.
Who says things will get better?

The monsoon hits hard. Helicopter
down, 600 rounds—if you please.

Fallen Warrior

Night falls upon us like a soaked quilt.
Somewhere in a cool computer room, in a glass
building, computer servers' eyes blink.

They gather like druids around a monolith,
around the fallen one. Tiresias.

The first generation server, the one
with semiconductors, the one created before
nanotechnology.

Servers blink on and off: red, green, red, red, red.
One by one they shut down, bringing the city down,

bringing the internet down,
in honor of Tiresias — the ancient one, generation one.

for Luis

Migrations

These migrations written on a khaki map,
from island lands, tales of hurricanes, red-billed parrots,
where phantoms jazz up the night in bebop
in the dust of flying stars, these spirits know no-nonsense,

know no borders, they bop over sacred seas.

World crossers of unknown lands, on shoulders they bear
palm crosses uprooted by singing breeze, that sweep
across waters, that carry their souls from tropical reefs to nations
upon nations on wounded wings of political winds.

No one can stop them, or anyone else can from entering nations,
not even if God wished it so.

Glorious

Today in the morning light,
I sit in a park, the wind whirls
around me. Branches sway

in the light. I dream angels. I see
angels.

I live in a hallucinatory world,
but the angels are real, curly haired
angels. Each angel I see elicits
in me a desire.

They look at me with their dark eyes.
I want to see something in their eyes,
something glorious, joyous,

a "yes," but I don't. I dream on,
and wait for the next one,

the next aeon, the next one, to carry on.

Voyager

on the great highlands
anxious like a hungry dingo
stalking a prey
for miles the soul migrates
from self to self
until in the twilight hours
you hear a howl in the wind
as she returns to the cosmos

Skyhawks

Tonight the night laments
Skyhawks
           takeoff from carriers
Why, then, do stars so brightly shine?

Late Night Fragments

***

Late at night, the moon backlights
city streets; her bright eyes,
like luminarias, guide our motorcars
safely to our separate homes.

***

In a cold desert town, missiles
demolish an abandoned dormitory,
artillery fires at an empty sky, soldiers
kneel to pray.

***

On the Calle de los Santos
where all the houses are painted pastel green,
a man named César sells grapes, speaks of inequality,
and of the fruits of the spirit.

***

At the end of the day, on Commerce Street,
a Pentecostal Church bell rings calling all
saints to Easter day.

***

Startled by nothing, silently,
Grackles on telephone lines scatter,
fly around a silver obelisk,
to celebrate the rising summer day.

Don Quixote's Tall Tales

O Lord, it is easier to live inside the world than outside the world.

I dreamt I was on an isolated beach with Don Quixote. I'm pretty sure it was a beach on the Atlantic Ocean. From where I stood, I could hear the waves slapping the jetty where a lone brown pelican hovered over the water, its fish pouch empty. But what astonished me most was what appeared to be in the distance the half-sunken body of the Statue of Liberty. Her blank face in despair, her torch bent slightly over to one side, worn down by the saline sea. A scene straight out of the *Planet of the Apes* where Charlton Heston played Taylor, an astronaut lost on an unknown planet, spots Lady Liberty, and says in agony, "You blew it up! Ah, damn you! God damn you all to hell!"

Then Don Quixote turned to me and said that Cervantes created his character, Don Quixote de la Mancha, from a scroll he found in a grotto beneath the darned forever-constructed *Basilica de la Sagrada Família*—Antoni Gaudi's masterwork. He swore to me that Miguel de Cervantes confessed to him he did not write the novel and that the Archangel Michael translated the scroll's hieroglyphs to him under duress.

This was hard for me to believe. Why would Archangel Michael dictate to Cervantes such a fantastical story? Then again, Michael was a well-seasoned warrior, with many battles underneath his belt.

I know how that goes; everybody has a novella or drama to tell. So maybe Archangel Michael was exercising his creative powers. Don Quixote also told me that he knew all along that the windmills were not ogres, but he felt sorry for Sancho Panza and so he just played along with Sancho to keep him alegre.

47

Anyway, Don Quixote had so many adventures to tell me that I knew he could go on for nights. But I was not a character in Scheherazade's untold Arabian stories, so I forced myself to wake up by thinking about how bad the traffic was on Highway 1604, and how much I valued my job especially after losing my good job as a fender assembler at the *maquiladora* in Juarez, run by los japonés. So there was no way that I was going to be late for work at Mama Margie's Mexican Restaurant.

Friday Morning

                  hours slip away;

the earth beneath my feet turns
to sand. Birds fly south.

A star implodes.
Cosmic rays adorn the sky.

Never a day passes without
the universe expanding,
contracting.

The auto shop opens at 7 a.m.
my car, in stasis—a cue ball
in line.

Late noon, the cat gets
VAXs at the Vet.

Conversations whiz by,
the TV is on the blips,
demonstrations flash by,

another window shattered
on Commerce Street...

THREE

THREE

El Demonio Likes Someone

I see dead people in my sleep. Recently, my brother
showed up, mi hermano, who passed away
at 52, the fastest fence climber at P.S. 61—a child
with more energy than a Lionel locomotive.

Who else could walk on his hands on East 12th Street?
The kids came from all around to watch him
do flips, stand at akimbo in the middle of the street
as the fire hydrant splashed off his naked chest.

A wild kid, a wild teen, conscripted by the Latin Dragons
—a warrior kicking a metal trash can down 110th street—
a crazy time, a crazy city, in the fifties. Later, a heavy smoker,
heavy drinker, a father,—gone now, a lost friend.

Yet he speaks to me in my sleep, like a spirit guide,
he warns me of impending doom and clear-cut opportunities.
Oddly enough, his consejos are dead wrong like the time he
advised me to buy a used green Gremlin from his friend, Paco.

That car turned out to be a driving disaster. And to think,
one time, I took that car across the border into Juarez.

It conked out on me after 35 miles into the border. A mustached
man flushed the radiator and the car started again. I made a U-turn,
headed straight back to the U.S. That ended my road trip into Mexico.

Bottom line: You cannot trust those nebulous figures in the night,
including your relatives. That possessed car took me through
undergraduate school, despite being vandalized several times
at the Calle Del Presidente.

It just would not die. I still have a picture of that car
which I called El Demonio in a shoebox in the far corner
of the attic where a raccoon keeps coming back.

Back to my brother, when the police found his body
outside a bar at Broward County, Florida; the first words
out of my mouth at 10:53 p.m. were "You asshole!"

Dear Brother, I shall never forget you, here, in this temperate
Texas day, when the dry snow rises into the quiet night;
until I, too, cease to be.

Last Ticket to Paradise

I seek a Temple of Light, an uninhabitable
zone, a place of rest, Aztlán, a forgotten
place, un paraíso—few know—an evergreen
space station, an exoplanet. I seek
yesteryear, future years, the purposelessness
of existence, contentment. We are star particles,
all of us. Today is the voyage.

Welcome to La Zona del Silencio,
terra ignota, the Mapimí Silent Zone,
Nazca, the sky desert, the ionosphere, dark
matter. Listen, no más. Now is the future.
The present is our ticket home.

Fast Talking Alien

Talk, talk, fast!

Who are you?
What do you want?

Violence is contagious.

What did you say?

Violence attracts violence.

Why should I care?

Violence breeds violence.

Blowing up others is an obsession.

Why do we worship our heroes?

Even successful soldiers grief.

La Maldición
(War: Apr 2, 1982 – Jun 14, 1982)

What pride what joy
to fly 7000 miles to bomb an island
to cross the mighty Atlantic
to fight a war

What pride what joy
it is to know that our country still
has the gumption to attack and pull back,
to sound the sirens, to call the troops,
to fight for naught in another land

What pride what joy
it is to defend and protect what needs
no protection, to kill and destroy,
to presume and assume an enemy,
because what feels like ours is not
theirs

What pride what joy to live the old lie:
Dulce y apropiado es morir por tu país

Dog Tales

> *"For God's sake, why don't you leave me the hell alone,*
> *and go back from where you came from?!"*

The Man at the Crossroads

The crooked man with the crooked legs waves a torn cardboard sign that reads, "Un Peso Por Favor." Some drivers throw a dollar onto his begging hand. Some people look straightaway, blasting their rumbas, speeding past the traffic light. Some say, he is a faker, an actor, like a wrestler. One cyclist claims, he saw him in a getaway car, a blue Corolla. I saw him too, but he wasn't driving.

One late day, I stepped up to him and asked, "Are you a veteran?"

He said, "I don't trust the Service. *Mira*. See these hands, combat engineer, that's what I did for them, dug trenches, walked the runway, cleared debris, explosives. Bomb Damage Assessment, BDM, that's what they called that job. That's why I move this way."

"See these dark twisted fingers, rheumatoid arthritis," the VA clinic, said.

"Have you gone back to the VA office? Maybe, there's someone there who can help you."

"Man, the government is a real bummer. Did you know they have tunnels everywhere in the city? The military put them there. They, the gov, come out at night like stinking rats. They watch me, all the time, cameras at every corner. The Service screwed up my paperwork. All they tell me is that the 'check is in the mail.' That was three years ago. I don't care anymore. I survived the desert; I can take care of myself."

After that talk, I drifted away, shaking my head thinking how truth gets in the way of life, especially when the truth shifts.

This world is crooked. To uncrook it, we have to take a sledgehammer to it.

To undo it, we have to uproot the rotten roots down to its rhizome. Get rid of the stockpile of bureaucratic manure, move the capital to the people.

But, before dismissing the unfortunate soul, I fumbled through my jacket, and found four loose dollars; I returned and handed them to Pablo.

Several days later like a lost ghost, I paced San Pedro Street back and forth searching for him. I never found him, except for a shattered soda bottle from wherewith he quenched his hungry soul.

In some ways, we are all crippled, somewhere.

Canton Jack
(Korean War Veteran)

Every morning I ease into my garden,
hold my wet finger to the air,

taste the weather. If it's fine

I struggle to my car drive to Corpus Christi,
and stare into the Gulf.

I flashback to Canton, where as a child
in Tian Square, I chased pigeons.

Years later after the Army,
I feel my muscles weaken,

English fades, Cantonese floods my brain.

I freeze to know that in the Republic of Texas
is where these bones will turn to ash.

Landstuhl Hospital
(Operation Iraqi Freedom)

Khalid is that you? Khalid Safi is that you?
In the landscape of dreamland, a voice calls Khalid.
He's nowhere found. Perhaps, he went back to Baghdad,

or sitting, right now, in a café in Istanbul sipping a cup
of Turkish coffee. He is not here. Here at Landstuhl Hospital,
I am not him, I tell the medical technician

who won't take no for an answer. I am in Germany,
eyes closed, curled up in a waiting room, waiting
for Doctor Cariño to see me. But, all I see

is the Texas landscape. I see my apartment. I see
El Paseo del Rio. I am not he, Khalid, the unknown one,
the missing one. Camp Sarafovo took its toll. I wait

for the technician to call me, to get my name right,
to see Doctor Cariño, to get better, to join the others
back in Camp Sarafovo to end this God-forsaken war.

Night Cross

After The Third of May 1808 (Francisco Goya, 1814)

Then the sky was filled with night.
In the distance, I saw a light
like no other.

I stood before a crowd of men,
some on their knees, others covering
themselves with their arms. Then

I extended my arms, palms opened
over my head, my body a wooden X.

In front of me stood a line of soldiers
with bayonets raised. Then I heard
and felt shots go through me.

In my risen body, I knew, I could
not save anyone, not this world,
not even me.

Death

Death is such a clown.
It pokes us. It slaps us
upside our heads, and says,
gotcha!

We feel the pain elsewhere.
Ouch! My darn back squeals.
My joints crack in agony.
We gripe.

But this devilish fool doesn't
exist. He is a reification,
a worm.

Our bladders exist, the earth
mother exists, what she says
goes.

Edwards Air Force Base

This wasn't yesterday or the day after, but the day the rain fell hard—little missiles ricocheting off the hangar walls. You could feel them, metallic drops, micro-cylinders, pelting the skin, rain

that flooded Rosamond Boulevard in the Mojave Desert.

The only street in this one-bird town that lead directly into the Base like a door on a mountain. The only time the huge fin appeared.

You could see it from the road sticking up on the dry lake a huge gray fin.

Next day the Mojave Express-News read, "Mammoth Shark Spotted in the Desert!" like a surprise party for a long-forgotten friend.

Grafenwoehr

1

We slept with our fatigues on, in sleeping bags zipped over our heads, like mummies in a crypt. Twenty men, twenty metal cots, in wooden barracks, no mattresses, no footlockers, no heat, no plumbing, temperature 38 degrees.

In the morning from a spigot on the side of a shed, we poured water into our helmets; we brushed our teeth, splashed cold water onto our faces, and shaved. After reveille, I got busy, as a medic, tending the sick.

At night, the artillery went on and on and on, armored personnel carriers disturbed the ground, tanks pounded the earth. One G.I., Private First Class Julio Roldan, took a nap under a deuce and a half, a two and half-ton, cargo truck. Never woke up—crushed by the 5,000-pound beast. The driver never knew it. The sad news rushed through the camp. After that, I slept facing the stars with one eye opened.

2

Detailed with a bunch of G.I.s to excavate a boulder that obstructed a dirt road, we dug in the mud for hours. Unable to unearth the monstrous rock, the Detail was called off—too tough for foot soldiers to manage. Hours later, a heavy vehicle with huge teeth pulverized the rock into a noxious gray pile. We hopped on the back of a camouflaged truck and got the hell out of there.

3

Who was in command? We never knew. For all we knew, the top dog might be Satan himself. It would be a miracle if we won this awful war. It would be another miracle for me to re-up. The battles would continue with or without us. We were not going anywhere. The war was not going anywhere. We were already there.

4

Months later, I went to see Dr. Dimasio at Heidelberg Hospital and recounted to him the Grafenwoehr incident. He asked me if I knew PFC Roldan. I told him I had met him once at the chow hall. Private Roldan was a slender guy from New Jersey with a pleasant tropical accent, like a cool summer's night. He had enlisted in the Army straight out of high school; that was all I knew. Dr. Dimasio prescribed Thorazine and sent me back to work.

Scar

Luigi's scar was a wrinkled trench
below his heart. He was quiet about
the marker left by a WWII bayonet.
The scar was the way his son,
Mario, made friends. He would invite
kids from down the block to see
his father's scar. His father would
grab his T-shirt and flip it high up
over his belly like a tent flap caught
on a spike. Squinting theirs eyes,
the kids would exam the scar
as if looking at a petrified mummy.
Mario would watch their faces, pick out
the ones with the silliest grins as buddies
then let the rest go.

Fallout

The moon is a skeleton. It's All Saints' Day. The zombie war won. Night rocks to normal. A baby cries. Dogs bark. A police car spotlight lights up the street.

Nearby, in an asphalt strip mall, shadowy figures in a low-tech store rewire motherboards. A lone straggler, by a lamppost, flicks a cigarette down a French drain.

The night screams. Two legs lie in an alleyway; a hand sticks out of a dumpster, fingernails polished green. Everywhere garbage trucks gather the dead.

Tomorrow is a holy day; no one goes to pray. No one will remember this, one hundred years from today.

Checking Out

Whether or not Christ descended to hell
only he can say. I can only speak for myself,
of my journey to Hades of the time the devil
stuck his finger into my cranium,

scrambled my brain. I ended up somewhere.
I cannot tell, I think, Colorado, maybe,
the Swedish hospital. I know not what I speak.

When I woke up the mirror on the wall
reflected a frown on my face.
I thought I was all right.

Still, I cannot distinguish whether
I had been to heaven or hell.
An aneurysm, I was told.

It is late now. Snow falls outside.

In the night, when I wake the Rockies melt
before me. I see fear on the moon's face.

My job is gone, now, somewhere inside the matrix.

Then I remember, my cubicle messy
as a city's landfill, my computer on the desk
so happy to see me in the morning, me playing
with the mouse, entertaining

Hamid a guy from the east, the guy

with the government calendar, who tallies
each day off before his retirement, 1001, 1000,
999 days. I'm checking out to check on him

to see if he's still counting. I'm not.

Physics

"You'll never amount to anything,"
my high school physics' teacher tells me.

As it turns out, he was right but wrong.
For all of us at the end will turn

to specks of anti-particles, positrons,
muonic dancers in electromagnetic fields.

But wrong he was. Because like the yin
and yang of the Tao-te Ching for every nothing

there is something, and that makes the world
go upside down, rightside up.

Gerszewski Barracks
(78th Engineer Battalion)

Pass the bowl, not the rice bowl,
but the bowl stashed with hash,
black Afghanistan, the good stuff,
said a frizzy hair soldier from Dallas,
as soldiers jostled each other,
played Spades, listened to Santana's
Hope You're Feeling Better,
laughed out loud, getting high
as endorphins kicked-in sending
them spinning to the funhouse,
while actually smoking camel crap.

Rockaway Beach

I have seen it happen. How waves
carry logs away. How waves submerge
rocks and docks.

How waves claw at the sand. How
the sand takes hit after hit, dissolves
into the sea.

How plovers run back and forth,
their needle feet

fleeing the fierce grip of the sea.
How heavy barges wind up
on land. Relentless, the turmoil tugs
and pulls like iron hands.

And if you turn your back the water
rises, drenches, your blanket, steals
your watch and wallet that you
have hidden in a plastic zip-lock

bag beneath the sand. And that poor
boy, you see, chasing the rainbow
beach ball. He, too, will soon
sink and cease to be.

Through the Window of the Taco Cabana

across the street of the all-night grocery store,
a man plays the saxophone. A man with a child
watches on.

And as if possessed by a spirit, the child begins
bobbing her head in the style jazz lovers
at an outdoor concert move to the bebop beats
on the Calle de la Luna.

When the spirit lets her go, the child quiets down.
The father holds her hand in the lamp-lit night,
and they wait for the next late bus home.

The musician continues to play under the spotlight
of the dim lamplight, where he sparkles like an earthlike
planet far away in a far-off galaxy.

By the house Allen built

across the motorway
pelicans brave the storm
no one suffers harm
whirlwinds tear billboards
verses raise the dead
minotaurs roam alleyways
people howl lyrical songs
till dawn

I cannot help but wonder
why I or my blue-eyed
cat is not there
versifying at the open mic
on the front lawn of the house
that Allen built

Army Veteran

I ask my daughter
do you want to look through the window.

She nods. We both look,
our heads pressed against a tiny porthole.

Inside, we see a bare concrete room.

On top of a conveyor belt sits a cardboard box.

I can only see one end.

I see my brother.

He wears a white gown that covers his shaved head.

He looks like a saint.

I see the side of his face,
his still black beard.

He is extremely serious.

I remember that look that expression, the one he
would give me when I borrowed his jacket

without asking.

My daughter's face turns away as the conveyor moves
into the blue-white flames.

Southwest Asia

She caresses her neck, almost signaling—
possibly an annunciation of some kind, a medal earned.

I stand at the checkout queue wondering about the mark
on her neck. I suspect

a stamp of involvement, a hickey. It's been years since
I thought about the word hickey. Then I think

about a soldier in the field somewhere in Southwest Asia
flying home.

His fingers fidget with a ribbon on his shirt, something to talk
about or something to forget.

I think about my own arrival home from Nam, how the world
has changed, how it has become not less dangerous,

but dangerous, nonetheless, unsafe in its own design.

Then all thoughts fade, the girl, the soldier,
as I step into the wires of the night.

The Room

I don't recognize the scribble. I didn't
write that. Yet something of me echoes

in what I see. It's been so long since I've
looked into that gray file cabinet. But there's

some truth written on a notepad there.
Like the sound of my daughter's voice

that once echoed at Carlsbad Caverns,
she said something about the dark,

and the humidity rose. What was it she said
that still resonates unintelligibly in my mind?

And what will she tell her boy that will resonate
for years to come like a fractured dream beckoning

to be recalled? What remains now is a cluttered room,
a dead Boom box that no one plays,

and a tennis racket in disrepair. On the wall,
the posters dangle dishearteningly; the room sits still

like the scribble on the pad, no longer useful or recognizable.

Empty.

FOUR

FOUR

Carlos

Praise to Carlos Ramos, mi primo,
who stumbled into life, spoke English,

Spanish, Italian, and German, before
he was nine, solved mathematical equations
of an unknown kind.

When company arrived, he stayed shut away
behind closed doors. Yet I could hear him wrestle
with Immanuel Kant.

He joined the Navy, sailed to Nanyang,
fell in love, ascended early speaking in tongues
to an unknown God.

Burnout

"The idea that dreaming is a normal kind of madness is not new."

— Dr. J. Allan Hobson

We are mad say, neuroscientists, all of us, in dreams. We walk invisible streets, move in psychotic states. We find ourselves flying through space, floating in the heavens. We are winged creatures—all of us.

In a dream, I am in Grand Central Station on a train. Beside me sits a woman reading *The Village Voice*. Who am I? What am I doing here? Where am I going? Why is that woman glaring at me?

Then I hear the conductor say, "Next stop! Delancey Street." I find myself in the Lower East Side, hair unkempt, lighting a cigarette, blowing smoke rings into the air, confetti rains down on me, as people board a space elevator. I move but cannot run. I speak but cannot hear.

We are mad, all of us. We become agitated, blood pressure up, hyperventilated,—streams of blips spike across an electroencephalograph. Then we relax, once again, we are in deep sleep, the journey disconnected. If we had been awake, we would be as mad as hell.

Sun Burial
(Canton Jack)

It is not a wicker picnic basket, definitely not placed
on a checkered blanket next to a Mesquite tree. No
sun tea soaking up the sun. No, this box is mahogany,
silver rails, with slick curvatures, draped with a flag.
On top of the box sits a picture of a man in his forties
in an Army uniform. The room is a ghost town except
for a woman with palms pressed together who bows
continuously before the picture. No one knows where
he will go. People trickle into the room. The woman slips
away. It is 102 degrees outside. A flock of geese heads east.

Interrogation Techniques
(Prisoner of War, Lt Col Salas)

We were alone
All of us

We were afraid

We knew that all of us
Would be singled out
One by one, interrogated
And tortured

In our cells at night
We tapped messages
To each other

From this, we learned
About the injured
The captured
The beatings

In our isolation some of us
Recited verses

Others imagined playing musical
Instruments or did long division
In our heads

Some faced a wall and spoke
To their families far away

Me, I became dead to the outside world

And learned how to sing silently
Within myself

As I wait my turn

The Old Man and the Guitar

An old blind man goes on a trip, perhaps, the tropics, maybe Vieques or even the island of Mona —stations for phantom migrations, souls traveling from elsewhere. On Mona, in a one-room museum, the curator recounts to the blind man the story behind a painting, a replica, of an old man with a guitar.

The man in the painting, blind from birth, gazes down deep into the earth; his long pale fingers cover the soundhole of the rosewood guitar, cross-legged his feet rest on the dirt floor. His brown skeletal shoulder exposed by his torn shirt.

Outside the museum, the curator tells the traveler about gypsy tunes, canto hondos, and boleros, the guitarist strum for tourists on Rivas Street—a street that slides down to the silence of the bay. Until one day, the guitar fades into the fog that consumes the shore.

Night Flight

The pilot flying his sky bright Cessna
over the Zone of Silence—a magnetic crater
saturated with space debris,

his instrument panel gone berserk,
finds himself in a misty mirrored room, where
the reflection of his lost father waves him on

In a corner of the room, a red eyeshadow parrot perched
on a cocoa tree picks ticks off its wings,

a gold ladder leans against a glass wall,
outside, cumulonimbus clouds darken.

Now, aimless in the Zone of Silence the pilot pushes
down on the steering wheel. Below on the ground,
he spots a runway strip.

He knows for sure the ground beneath
him is as solid as the blinking star Canopus,

which lies in the constellation of Carina
that in Latin means ship,

which guided ancient seafarers home
after a long journey on the yet unexplored sea.

Hero

One day you are in Las Vegas
at the Sahara Hotel chomping down
on a half-pound filet mignon,

and the next day at home, you are talking
to Dr. Sanchez about acid reflux. He says
come down to the VA Hospital.

So you go,
as it turns out you have a heart condition,
and so they insert a stent in your heart—

a foreign object, something that is not
part of your anatomy,

and your dream of retiring to the Yucatan fades.
The fútbol game of Mexico versus Argentina
is on the tube. You watch the game and you see

the guys running back and forth chasing the ball
on the field that reminds
you of how much you chased

money around—now lying on the hospital
bed, you think, how *time* now is the hero
you'll chase more than anything else.

The Lieutenant

He did it for glory.

He did it for the mission.

He did it for faith.

He did it for his comrades.

He did it for his country.

He massacred the village

to no blessed end.

Davis–Monthan AFB

Plane graveyard in the Sonoran Desert
Played out military insignias on fighter jets
Tires flat Wings down Tails static
No nose art visible No pretty girls
In mint/yellow polka dots bikinis
"Quick—Inhale deeply," said Miguel,
As smoke clouds of confiscated hashish
Raced towards the runway

Richport

It's hard for me to stand
To walk any line
To unspeak the unspeakable

I don't know if I am dreaming or dying

La Tormenta, the storm, slashed rich port,
Puerto Rico, Borinquen, without mercy

It's gushing blood

To think, simple rain and wind,
All things beautiful torn asunder

Put aside, lifted up,

Watchtowers, human selves,
Roadways, doorways,
Kids, mercados, clinicas,

Cars, families, mi gente,
Colony, Island of Enchantment,

Isla del Encanto,

Estados Unidos, United States,
Us, them, you, them, where, *their*

History—an iron sky

Highway 15 West

I was leaving Barstow Marine Base in California on Highway 15 West, heading to Mojave Air Base when I fell behind an 18-wheeler that was going uphill and grunting like an old rhinoceros.

In my disquietude, I proceeded to pass this slow-moving mammal. As I struggled through clouds of smoke and dust, my car swerved just a wee bit onto the gravel shoulder, but I came out unscathed from the ordeal except for a rogue hubcap that aped away clanking across the road.

Shortly, after that insane incident, I noticed from my rear-view mirror flashing blue and red lights swooping down on me like a starving Pterodactyl.

Thank God! It was just CHIP, the California Highway Patrol, not the ugly flesh-eating creature. Maybe, the nice officer was going to inquire about the clanking hubcap.

Sir, the State Trooper asked me, did you just pass an 18-wheeler on the right-hand side? No, sir, I said. I would never do that. I thought I saw you pass it, he said.

No, sir, the truck slowed down and I simply moved to the right to get out of its way—the truck fell behind me.

Okay, said the officer, in that case, have a nice day. Thank you, sir, I said, as I squirreled away.

The Accident

My mother misses me.
I know she does. She keeps my picture
on the bookcase, on the high shelf,

in the living room, higher than the lamps open
like white lilies that stare beyond
the vaulted ceiling.

A cat has nine lives, I know.
Do nine lives equal, nine earth-years?
Nine years, I lived there.

What's left now is a picture of me
high on the bookcase.

In El Salvador, the rain
washed away the road, the car spun out of control,
crashed through the rail; the caretaker, the driver,
floated, spun, descended,

as in a dream, down,
down, bouncing, as if on a trampoline, all the way
down to the riverfront.

An aunt, in a small town,
keeps a secret about me, a newsprint stowed away,
a photo of me—Consuelita,

a piece there and there of me,
and the caretaker, still strapped to her seat,
as in a lucid dream.

Frail Experiment

I make something out of nothing—a house
out of toothpicks, a boy from nickel wire,
lightning from honey, arsenic from history.

You see, I have this pinched
nerve like Paul's thorn in the flesh,

that takes me home,
to scientific love, frail experiments, paradise,

—fragmented like Chagall's art.

It triggers my art that I toil for seven days
a week, an affliction that keeps coming back

like crabgrass each summer. But I
love my art; my life is a marvelous mess,
like stars falling from paradise.

Arrival

They came from no place,
yet somewhere. Some say
a distant galaxy, night phantoms,
spirits, which lit the sky.
The earth tilted.
They came from a future time, we supposed.
We covered our faces, locked our ears,
inquired about light travel, wormholes, quantum fields,
stood in desperation.
Their spherical spaceship, gray shapes
against an orange sky,
said nothing of their travels.
In hollow voices, a message arrived,
we are searching for heaven.
We had no answers for these landless creatures.
And, as easy as twilight arrived, their starship disappeared.
Homeless, they left without their wish,
their dreams ahead.

Chorus

This is the end. Almost anything can
happen. A mural of an angel is being
drawn on the wall of the Capitol, and
we have not yet begun to pray.

If I have to live, it will be without rudder and in delirium.

— **Gilberto Owen**

Biography

Dario Beniquez was born in Aguadilla, Puerto Rico, and raised in Far Rockaway, NY. He is a poet and engineer. He is an Army veteran and lives in San Antonio, Texas. For over 23 years, he has facilitated the Gemini Ink Literary Arts Center Open Writers' Workshop, which is free to the San Antonio community. He, also, facilitates the *Voices del la Luna Literary Magazine* poetry workshop, which he established. He holds a BEIE from Pratt Institute, Brooklyn, NY; M.P.A., and M.S. in Industrial Engineering, from New Mexico State University, Las Cruces, NM; and an MFA from Pacific University, OR. His poetry has been published in The Brave: a Collection of Poetry and Prose, Red Palm Poetry Magazine, TEJASCOVIDO Literary Journal, San Antonio Express-News, Chrysalis Literary Journal, Mesquite Review, The Texas Observer, Mojave Desert News, di-vêrsé-city, Austin International Festival Anthology; VIA Poetry on the Move Anthology, the Caribbean Writer, Kuikatl, 30 Poems for the San Antonio Tricentennial Anthology, I Had Once Seen Anthology, San Pedro Creek Poetry Anthology—San Antonio River Authority, El Placazo, Humble Pie Literary Magazine, Rio Grande Review, McNay Art Museum, Exhibit: "Robert Indiana: A Legacy of Love," Unstrung Poetry Magazine, and elsewhere.

CPSIA information can be obtained
at www.ICGtesting.com
Printed in the USA
LVHW090756020323
740531LV00030B/258

9 781953 447814